NATURE IN THE NEIGHBORHOOD

GORDON MORRISON

Houghton Mifflin Company Boston 2004

Walter Lorraine Books

"To my nine brothers and sisters with love, and memories of the neighborhood of our time."

Author's Note

Where can you find nature?

In forests, on mountains, in deep valleys, and faraway places? Yes, all true. But where else can you find it?

Everywhere! It sprouts at your feet, scurries through the grass, scampers up a tree, or flies across the sky. Nature is the changing seasons, the rain that falls from the clouds, and the leaf drifting through the air. It is all of this and more. And it's all in your neighborhood.

I grew up in a city neighborhood. As a child I knew very little about nature. As an adult I have sketched and observed nature and traveled to many places, some far away. But many of my sketches were done from my window, or in my yard, or around my neighborhood. You don't have to travel far to find nature. Just stop wherever you are and take the time to look, nature is there. Be curious, look out your window, step out your door, or walk around your neighborhood. Remember, it doesn't matter whether you live in the city or the country, because nature is everywhere.

—G.M.

Walter Lorraine (wr) Books

Copyright © 2004 by Gordon Morrison

www.houghtonmifflinbooks.com

Library of Congress Cataloging-in-Publication Data

Morrison, Gordon.
    Nature in the neighborhood / Gordon Morrison.
        p. cm.
    ISBN 0-618-35215-5
    1. Natural history—Juvenile literature. 2. Seasons—Juvenile literature. I. Title.
    QH48.M864 2004
    508—dc22

                                                    2004002354

ISBN–13: 978-0-618-435215-9

Printed in the United States of America
WOZ   10 9 8 7 6 5 4 3 2 1

On the sidewalk by an alley, the warm sun melts the last patches of snow. Water from the melting snow trickles into a crack. Soil in the crack gets wet and softens. Tiny roots from a seed spread in the soil, and a small plant begins to grow. Spring is returning to the neighborhood.

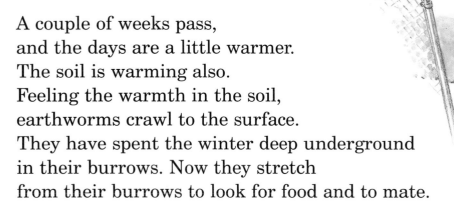

A couple of weeks pass,
and the days are a little warmer.
The soil is warming also.
Feeling the warmth in the soil,
earthworms crawl to the surface.
They have spent the winter deep underground
in their burrows. Now they stretch
from their burrows to look for food and to mate.

Earthworm, to 8 inches long. A segmented, soft-bodied animal that can compress or extend its body.

Burrowing, digging: pushing its pointed head into the earth, it stretches and then expands its body, forcing the soil apart. When worms burrow into hard soil, they eat through it.

When grabbed, a worm expands its body, and pairs of tiny bristles on each body segment dig into the soil, holding it tightly to the burrow wall. If the tail breaks off, the worm escapes and grows a new one.

A small flock of birds lands on the lawn of the Jackson Elementary School. They are male robins returning from the south. Tired and hungry, they look for worms and insects. In a week or two the female robins will return. Then the males will sing *cheer-up, cheer-up, cheerily* to attract the females— a sure sign that spring has returned to the neighborhood.

Aboveground a worm eats fresh grass and leaves and decaying plant and animal matter. Belowground it eats plant and animal matter while burrowing.

Castings are balls of undigested earth and plants, or waste, found on the ground. They make excellent fertilizer.

It's dusk—
that time when day is just ending
and night has not yet begun
and when streetlights come on.
Baseball season has started.
Above the field, two birds roll
and sweep across the sky, catching insects.
Their white wing patches flash in the light of dusk.
They are nighthawks. They have come to the
neighborhood to live and to raise a family.

Nighthawk, 12 inches long.
It may look like a hawk when
it flies, but it is not a hawk.

Nighthawks have tiny beaks
and big mouths for
catching flying insects.
Their feet are small
for perching on flat surfaces.
They build no nest but lay
their eggs on the ground
or on a gravel rooftop.

Hawks have large, sharp beaks
for tearing flesh and large feet
with talons for holding prey.
They build nests of twigs and
branches, usually in a tree.
Hawks do not usually fly at
night. Nighthawks usually do.

Other night flyers:
Chimney swift, 5 inches:
Cigar-shaped high flyer that glides
between stiff, rapid wingbeats.
Nests in chimneys.

Little brown bat, to 4 inches:
Bats are the only true flying
mammals. Their flight is low and
fluttering with abrupt turns
and twists. They roost in
caves, buildings, or attics.

Four weeks have passed since the robins returned.
The female robins have been very busy. They have built nests
in trees and shrubs and on windowsills and fire escapes. One
even built her nest in an open alarm box, where she
laid four eggs. For two weeks she incubated them,
sat on the eggs to keep them warm and dry.
Three days ago the babies hatched.
The male robin guards the nest area.
He also helps feed the young birds.
Young robins grow fast.
In about twelve days they
will fly from the nest.

All three night flyers are
insectivores, or insect eaters.
They eat lots of mosquitoes,
moths, flying ants, beetles,
flies, and other insects.

7

On a little hill behind the school an old red oak tree stands.
From a large limb hangs a rope swing. From smaller branches
the oak's flowers hang, and new leaves are growing.
A gray squirrel gathers oak leaves. She has four babies
in a leaf nest high above the rope swing. They are six weeks old.
She will add the leaves to the nest to keep them warm and dry.
Nearby is a rock outcrop, a climbing
rock where children play.

In the dry oak leaves
around the rock some plants grow.
They are called Solomon's seal.
Solomon's seal flowers bloom before
the growing oak leaves block the sunlight.

Outcrop: the part of bedrock that shows
above the ground. Bedrock is solid rock
that is under all the soil and other material
on the earth's surface.

Solomon's seal was named
for Solomon, the tenth century
B.C. king of Israel. His wax
seal was a six-pointed star.
The plant's root scars look like
wax seals, and its flowers
have six points.

Weeks pass.
The days are getting
warmer. In the alley
a gentle breeze
freshens wash hung
out to dry. A family
of mourning doves
perches on the
clothesline. Their slow,
mournful, sad-sounding call
—*coo-ah, coo, coo, coo*— gave them their name.
The young doves have just left the nest. Their
fluffy new feathers make them look bigger
than their parents. One of the adults flies away.
Its wings make a whistling
sound when it flies.

Mourning dove, 12 inches:
Doves are members of the pigeon
family. But *pigeon* usually refers
to stocky birds with broad tails,
dove to slender birds
with long, pointed tails.

Back in the oak tree,
the leaves have grown big
and are spreading. Clusters
of small acorns appear where the
flowers used to be.
The young squirrels are now big enough
to leave their nest. They are nine weeks old.
But they must be careful not to fall.
So they cling to the oak and stay
close to their mother. They have a lot to learn
about climbing, running, and leaping.

Doves pair for life. Both parents raise the young.
And both feed "pigeon milk," a
curdlike secretion produced inside
a part of the neck called the crop,
to the nestlings.

The male dove gathers twigs, and
the female builds a flimsy platform
nest, often in an evergreen tree.
They usually have two
broods of two young,
but may have up to five
broods in the south.

Doves eat seeds from many
different grasses and weeds.

In an empty lot where a house used to be, many weeds grow.
Crabgrass spreads in a gravel path. It's the same plant that grows in
the crack of the sidewalk. Bromegrass gently bobs and sways
in the wind. Fescue grass stands tall and straight.
Red clover and white clover creep around the other plants.
Some milkweed plants have many flower buds.
Others don't have any yet. Curled dock has curly
leaves and lots of tiny green flowers.
And field thistle is covered with sharp spines.
Its flower buds are just starting to show.

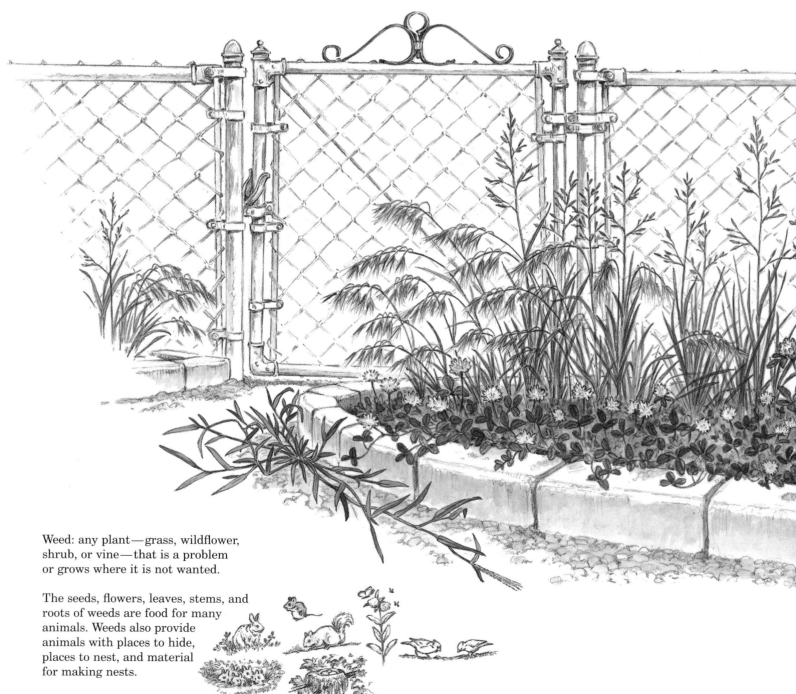

Weed: any plant—grass, wildflower,
shrub, or vine—that is a problem
or grows where it is not wanted.

The seeds, flowers, leaves, stems, and
roots of weeds are food for many
animals. Weeds also provide
animals with places to hide,
places to nest, and material
for making nests.

A cottontail rabbit is raising her second family. In a nest lined with her soft fur, she gave birth to five bunnies. She has nursed them since they were born two weeks ago. Now a bold little bunny looks out from the plants. It is the first to leave the nest. Over the next few days, one by one, the other bunnies will leave. Soon they will be on their own.

Several weeks go by.
The days are very warm.
Curled dock flowers are gone now.
Clusters of winged seeds fill their stems.
Field thistle has grown to eight feet tall.
Some flowers are open. More will bloom
through the summer. Milkweeds are
heavy with blossoms. But on some plants
the flowers are gone and seed-
pods are beginning to grow.

The monarch's entire life cycle is
connected to the milkweed:
Tiny eggs, $\frac{1}{32}$ inch long,
are laid on milkweed leaves.
Three days later, $\frac{1}{8}$-inch-long
caterpillars chew their way out of
the eggs and eat the leaves.

In four weeks they shed their
skin four times and grow
to 2 inches. Then they spin a silk thread,
hang by it, and form a chrysalis.
Ten or twelve days later, butterflies
emerge. Living only two weeks,
they feed, mate, and lay their
eggs on milkweed leaves.

Summer is here. Monarch butterflies flutter around the milkweed
plants and sip nectar from the flowers. The first butterflies arrived
several weeks ago. They laid their eggs on the milkweed
leaves. When the tiny caterpillars hatched they began eating
the leaves. For about four weeks they ate, and ate,
and ate. Now they stop eating. They are big, plump caterpillars.
Some hang upside down from the plants. Soon a new
skin covering, called a chrysalis, will form around them.
Inside the chrysalises the caterpillars will pupate, change.
Slowly they will become butterflies. Then the chrysalises
will split open and the butterflies will push out.
For several hours they will hold on to the plants
until their beautiful wings spread.
Then they will fly away.

Other milkweed visitors:
Sphinx moths visit at dusk and
sip nectar with their long tongues.

Honeybees and bumblebees
collect pollen from the flowers.

Milkweed bugs eat seeds from the
pods. This bug's entire life cycle
is also connected to the milkweed.

Garter snake, 18–26 inches:
the most commonly seen snake.
It mates in early spring, and by
midsummer twelve to forty live
young are born. It is not dangerous,
but it does have a painful bite.
Food, eaten whole, includes
earthworms, slugs, insects,
spiders, toads, frogs, birds,
eggs, and small mammals.

A spider look-alike and relative:
daddy longlegs, eight 2-inch legs.
The head and body form one part.
It has no silk to spin a web. It hunts
among grasses and weeds. Eggs are
laid in the ground or under debris.

Long-legged spider: eight 2-inch legs
and two body parts. Makes a web
under porches and in cellars. Eggs
develop in a sac carried by the female.

Note: Insects have six legs and three
body parts.

Honeybees and bumblebees buzz around a neighbor's garden. Flowers
and shrubs bloom. Leaf lettuce grows thick in a row. Tomatoes and
pole beans grow up a twig trellis. And bright sunflowers nod their heads.
A garter snake coils in the shade to keep cool on a hot summer day.
A garden spider waits in its orb, or "round," web for an insect to get
caught. A daddy longlegs scurries along the ground, hunting.
Luckily it is not seen by a plump toad sitting nearby.
The toad sits with its eyes closed,
soaking up water from a dripping hose.

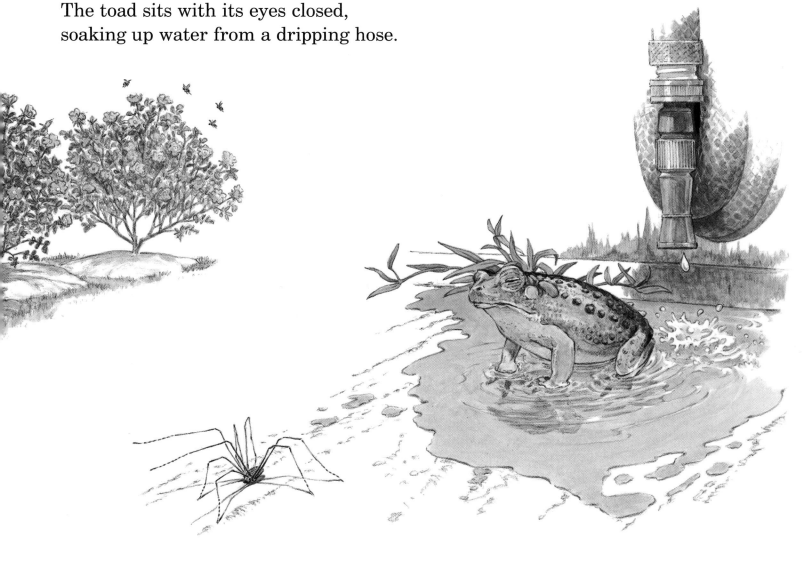

American toad, to 3¹/₂ inches.
Toads are amphibians, living part
of their life in water (as tadpoles)
and part on land. They "drink" by
absorbing water through their dry skin.
They shed their warty skin and eat it.
Warts are poisonous to some enemies.
Toads thrust their sticky tongues out
2 inches to catch their food.

Toads eat earthworms, ants,
spiders, daddy longlegs,
slugs, flies, mosquitoes,
and small animals.

On a flat gravel rooftop, near the ball field, the nighthawks are raising two chicks. The female sits with her back to the sun. She covers and shades her ten-day-old chicks. In another twenty days, the young birds will leave the nest.

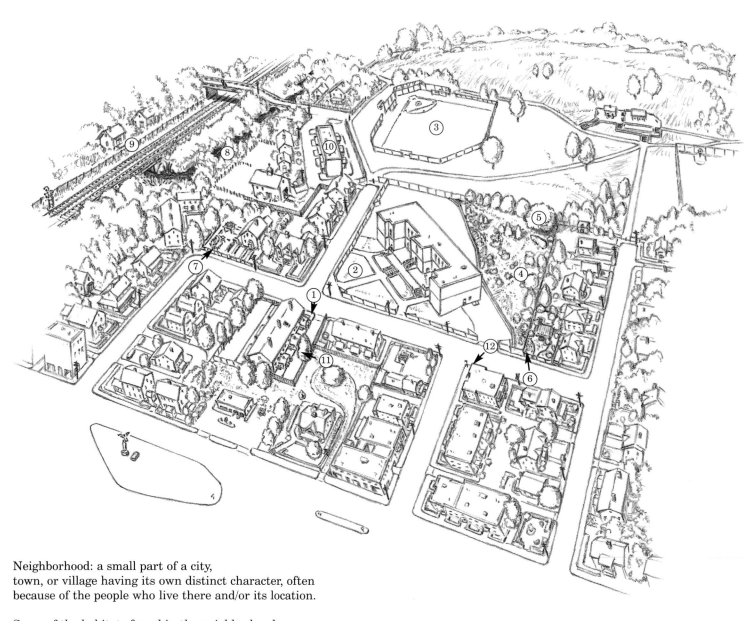

Neighborhood: a small part of a city, town, or village having its own distinct character, often because of the people who live there and/or its location.

Some of the habitats found in the neighborhood:

1. Sidewalk by alley
2. School lawn
3. Ball field
4. Little hill
5. Red oak tree
6. Empty lot
7. Garden
8. Riverside corridor
9. Railroad corridor
10. Rooftop with nighthawk nest
11. Spruce tree where doves nest
12. Alarm box and robins' nest

Three young rabbits have found their way into the garden.
Their mother is back in the empty lot, raising a third family.
These rabbits are eight weeks old now. Soon they may have
families of their own. For now they just
want to nibble on fresh lettuce leaves.

Habitat: a place where animals or
plants have what they need to survive.

Animals need food, water, and
shelter and places to hide, to build
nests, and to raise families.

Plants need the right soil,
the right amount of moisture,
and seasonal changes
in light and temperature.

A habitat could be a large area,
like a forest, with many places for
many different plants and animals.

It could be a small area, like a
neighborhood, where some
animals find what they need
in different places.

Or a habitat could be a
riverside, where certain plants
need water to grow in or near.

A habitat could be very small,
like a garden, where a bird nests
in a shrub and other plants
provide it with food and safety.

Other neighborhood plants and animals:

Blue jay: a noisy year-round resident that may nest in cedar trees.

Dandelion: in French its name, *dent de lion,* means "tooth of the lion" because of its sharp-edged leaves.

White-footed mouse: may move into a home in winter but goes back outdoors in spring.

White spruce, to 75 feet: with long, hanging cones. An ideal place for mourning doves to nest.

Blue flag, to 4 inches wide: a beautiful blue flower that grows along a marshy edge of a river.

Dragonflies are much bigger than their relatives, the damselflies, but both hunt along the river.

Raccoon: sleeps in trees during the day, rattles trash cans by night.

Little black ants: there may be 40,000 ants in a colony, all the children of a single queen.

Marigold: bright yellow flowers, grows in shallow, slow water in springtime.

Cardinal: male is bright red; female, brownish. In winter visits yards but feeds on the ground.

Band-winged grasshopper, 1 inch: color bands on the hind wings show when it flies.

Gray tree frog, 2½ inches: breeds in water in spring. In summer climbs trees and sings its birdlike trill.

Phoebe, 7 inches: flicks its tail when perching, sings its name, *fee-bee,* and often nests near people.

Woolly bear: common black and brown caterpillar seen crossing roads in the fall.

Red cedar tree, to 50 feet: with small bluish cones and dense foliage for hiding and nesting.

Chickadees, tufted titmice, and downy woodpeckers form a small flock in winter and visit feeders.

Deer and sometimes even moose enter neighborhoods, having traveled unseen through corridors.

Ragweed's green flowers and windblown pollen cause hay fever. Goldenrod's yellow flowers are pollinated by insects.

Swoosh!
Something flies down, trying to catch a rabbit.
The rabbits leap out of the way. They run and hop
as fast as they can to hide in the plants.
It is a hunting bird, a small falcon called a kestrel.
It has caught other bunnies during spring and summer.
But these rabbits have grown too big
and are too fast to be caught. So the kestrel
flies away to hunt someplace else.
Lucky for them, the kestrel did not see the toad
by the hose or the snake in the shade.

Kestrel, 9 to 12 inches:
often sits on wires or poles
and hovers over open spaces, hunting.
Its loud call, *klee-klee-klee,* carries a
long distance. They nest in cavities
in buildings or trees or in
boxes built for them.

The kestrel's larger relative,
the peregrine falcon, may dive
at speeds near 200 miles an hour.

The kestrel eats mostly
mice, but also
young rabbits
and squirrels,
snakes, toads,
insects, and
birds.

In late summer, when hot days begin to cool, thistle flowers turn to seeds. And when most birds have finished raising their families, goldfinches begin to raise theirs. The female makes the nest. She may build it high in a tree or close to the ground. She may even build it among thistle plants.

American goldfinch, 5 inches:
Finches are also called seed-eaters, because
their bills are cone-shaped for cracking seeds.
They eat seeds of thistle, grass, goldenrod, aster, sunflower,
dandelion, and some tree, shrub, and garden flower seeds.
A small amount of berries and insects are also eaten.

Thistle seeds have a soft tuft called down. The down acts as a parachute, helping the seeds drift away on the wind. Goldfinches eat the seeds and line their nests with thistle down. Baby goldfinches are only fed mushy thistle seeds. Their parents partially eat the seeds to make them soft. In seven days the young birds will leave the nest. They will be two weeks old and able to eat whole seeds from thistle and other plants. Milkweed pods are growing. Grass seeds are ripe. And curled dock leaves are colored with blotches of red and brown.

The female weaves the nest, usually in a fork of a tree or a shrub, near a thistle seed supply. She lays four to six eggs. The male may feed her while she incubates them. Both raise the nestlings, and both regurgitate partially digested thistle seeds into the young birds' mouths, slowly adding whole seeds as the birds grow.

23

Asters and goldenrods are blooming. A garter snake has shed its skin and left it tangled at the base of the plants. Baseball season is coming to an end. The days are getting shorter and cooler. The nighthawks are leaving the neighborhood. They have raised their family—during the summer the young birds learned to fly and to catch insects. Now they are full grown. So all four birds fly into the sky and head south to warmer places.

Monarch butterflies are also starting their long journey south. But these are not the same butterflies that pushed out from their chrysalises in early summer. That was about six weeks ago, and they lived only a few weeks. But their caterpillar offspring grew and changed into these butterflies. And these butterflies are special. They will live for nine months and somehow know to fly all the way to Mexico to spend the winter.

Following the milkweed, an incredible journey: In early spring millions of Monarch butterflies fly north from the Sierra Madre in central Mexico (1). Reaching Texas or Louisiana (2), they reproduce, lay their eggs on emerging milkweed plants, then die, having lived for nine months. Three generations follow, each moving northward (3) with the emerging milkweed, but each lives only a few weeks. In early summer the third generation reaches their northern homes (4).

There, in southern Canada and the northeastern United States, two more generations mate, lay eggs on milkweed, and live only a few weeks. But a third generation does not reproduce. And in early fall these butterflies migrate (5) 1,500 miles back to the Sierra Madre and mass together to spend the winter in semi-dormancy. In spring they complete the cycle by flying north, having lived for nine months.

Across the neighborhood, railroad tracks run beside a river. The kestrel hunts along these tracks. It has caught a mouse. A coyote also hunts here. It hunts for mice and larger animals, like rabbits and squirrels. The thick growth of shrubs and trees along the river and tracks makes secret places for children to have forts. It also makes a corridor, a place where even large animals like deer and coyote are hidden.

Coyote, 4 feet long, including tail. Coyotes breed in midwinter. Four or five pups are born in spring. Both the male and female raise the pups.

Coyotes eat mostly mice, but their diet includes rabbits, squirrels, birds, fish, raccoon, deer, insects, carrion (dead animals), garbage, grass, seeds, and fruits.

Coyotes look like German shepherds but are usually smaller, with a long-legged look. Coyotes carry their tails down. Dogs carry their tails up. Coyotes' tracks are fairly straight. Dogs' zig-zag. Coyotes' prints are oval, with two nails showing. Dogs' are rounder, with toes spread and four nails showing.

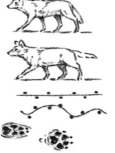

In the gravelly railroad bank, scouring rush grows. Native Americans used the rough stems to scour cooking utensils. In the river, cattail plants grow eight feet tall. Hundreds of tufted seeds form the soft, downy "cattails" at the top of the stem. Hay-scented ferns carpet a sunny spot along the river's edge. Their crushed fronds smell like hay. And vines of riverbank grape reach out over the water. The ripe fruit fills the air with its sweet scent. After the first frost, the grapes will be ready for eating.

Corridor: a narrow passageway or place connecting one neighborhood or woodland to another, where animals may pass unseen. It could be anything from a tree line through a meadow to a ravine through a city.

Fall has arrived.
Plants are changing color,
and animals are getting ready for winter.
Milkweed leaves turn bright yellow, then pale yellow.
Curled dock leaves are a dull chocolate brown. Many have fallen.
Thistle plants' colors are fading to gray.
And red oak acorns are ripe and falling.
The squirrel is raising her second family.
They eat lots of acorns and bury many
more for a winter food supply.
During the summer the robins also raised a
second family. All grown now, they know
it is time to leave. The days are getting cold,
so they gather in a small flock
and fly from the neighborhood.

Several weeks pass. Most plants have changed color. The red oak tree
is one of the last to change. Its leaves turn crimson red. Soon they will
fall. A frost is due any day now. Garter snakes curl up together in spaces
under rocks or in foundation walls to hibernate through the winter.
The toad digs a deep, underground burrow in soft soil,
where it will sleep until spring returns.
A flock of geese flies in V formation, heading south.
Their honking calls can be heard as they pass over the neighborhood.

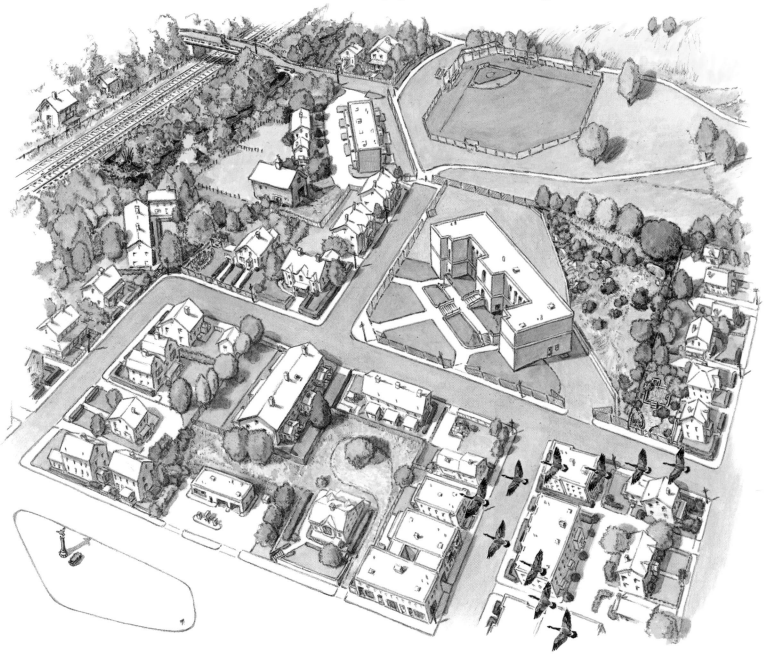

All reptiles and amphibians, including snakes and toads, are said to be cold-blooded. This really means
that they cannot make their own body heat. They are as warm or as cold as the air around them. To get warm
they lie in the sun on rock walls or roadways. To get cool they crawl into the shade among rocks and plants.
To survive the long, cold winter, snakes gather under rocks or in empty burrows, and toads dig burrows to 3
feet deep. Then they stop or slow their body processes and go into a deep sleep, called dormancy.

The day is bright and sunny after a fresh snowfall. Sunflowers hang from the twig trellis in the garden. The lettuce, tomatoes, and beans are gone. Bird feeders stand in their place. Squirrels and mourning doves eat seeds scattered on the snow. Neighborhood birds pick seeds from the sunflowers and the feeders. In their winter feathers, the male and female goldfinches look alike. In the empty lot, on the little hill, along the river, and in neighborhood yards, animals can find lots to eat.

How plants survive winter: Some plants, like milkweed, die completely, leaving their seeds to grow into new plants the next year.

Others, like hay-scented fern, die back to the ground, but belowground their roots survive to grow again.

And some, like the oak, send their sap (water and nutrients) down to their roots to keep from freezing. In the spring, the sap rises up into the plant and it grows again.

It's late winter. There is no school today. A heavy snow blankets the neighborhood. More snow is falling. Dry milkweed pods and curled dock seeds sway on leafless stalks. In shrubs and trees, under porches and roof overhangs, animals find shelter from the storm. But tracks in the snow show that rabbits have been out of their dens and a coyote may have passed this way.

Deep snow acts as a blanket, insulating and protecting plants and animals from sudden temperature changes.
It also provides a cover from predators for some animals, like mice.

On the sidewalk and in the alley, snow is still piled high.
But the days are getting a little longer and a little warmer.

Soon the last patches of snow will melt. The soil will warm and soften.
Small seeds will spread their roots. Earthworms will stretch from their
burrows. And robins will sing, *cheer-up, cheer-up, cheerily.*
Then spring, once again, will return to the neighborhood.